LOVE PUPPIES

Copyright © 2008 Sellers Publishing, Inc.

Photography © 2008 Jane Burton &
Mark Taylor/Warren Photographic

Sellers Publishing, Inc.
P. O. Box. 818, Portland, Maine 04104

For ordering information:

(800) 625-3386 toll-free

(207) 772-6814 fax `

Visit our Web site: www.rsvp.com • E-mail: rsp@rsvp.com

ISBN 13: 978-1-4162-0518-0

Printed and bound in China.

Please note: Every attempt has been made to contact current copyright holders when
appropriate. Any omission is unintentional and the publisher welcomes hearing from any
copyright holders not acknowledged. Omissions will be corrected in subsequent printings.

Dedication

For all love puppies everywhere

LOVE PUPPIES

My Heart Belongs to You

SELLERS
PUBLISHING

Follow

your bliss.

— JOSEPH CAMPBELL

You may not be the brightest bulb in the socket, but without you I'd be in the dark.

God created the flirt as soon as he made the fool.

– VICTOR HUGO

*All females are flirts, but some
are restrained by shyness,
and others by sense.*

– FRANÇOIS DE LA ROUCHEFOUCAULD

Look at that!
Look how she moves!
That's just like Jello-O on springs.

– SOME LIKE IT HOT
UNITED ARTISTS PICTURES, 1959

Love may be blind,
but it sure can find its way
around in the dark!

– AUTHOR UNKNOWN

I think every girl is looking
for her Mr. Darcy.

– KEIRA KNIGHTLEY

Love has nothing to do with what you are expecting to get — only with what you are expecting to give — which is everything.

– KATHARINE HEPBURN

*If you can make a girl laugh
— you can make her do
anything . . .*

— MARILYN MONROE

A kiss is a lovely trick designed by nature to stop speech when words become superfluous.

– INGRID BERGMAN

To me, there is no greater act
of courage than being the
one who kisses first.

– JANEANE GAROFALO

If it is your time, love will track you down like a cruise missile.

— LYNDA BARRY

*I'd love to kiss you but
I just washed my hair.*

– CABIN IN THE COTTON

WARNER BROTHERS, 1932

As for kissing on the first date, you should never date someone whom you would not wish to kiss immediately.

– GARRISON KEILLOR

Kisses are a better fate than wisdom.

— E. E. CUMMINGS

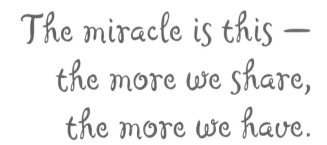

The miracle is this —
the more we share,
the more we have.

– LEONARD NIMOY

Life is short. Be swift to love!

– HENRI F. AMIEL

If you love someone say it;
you say it right then, out loud.
Otherwise, the moment just
passes you by…

– MY BEST FRIEND'S WEDDING

SONY PICTURES ENTERTAINMENT
AND TRISTAR PICTURES, 1997

When we are in love we seem
to ourselves quite different from
what we were before.

– BLAISE PASCAL

I love you.
I've loved you since the first
moment I saw you. I guess
maybe I've even loved you
before I saw you.

– A PLACE IN THE SUN
PARAMOUNT PICTURES, 1951

One is very crazy
when in love.

– SIGMUND FREUD

*With my brains
and your beauty,
we're a perfect match.*

— YIDDISH SAYING

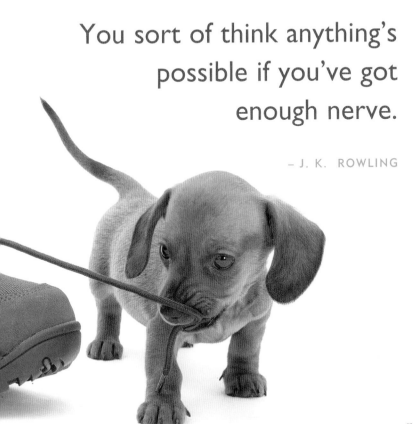

You sort of think anything's possible if you've got enough nerve.

– J. K. ROWLING

51

Laughter is the shortest distance between two friends.

– VICTOR BORGE

It's not the having,
it's the getting.

– ELIZABETH TAYLOR

What the world really
needs is more love
and less paperwork.

– PEARL BAILEY

There is no living with thee, nor without thee.

– MARCUS VALERIUS MARTIAL

Here's looking at you, kid.

– CASABLANCA

WARNER BROTHERS, 1942

You know you're in love when you can't fall asleep because reality is finally better than your dreams.

— DR. SEUSS

Nobody has ever measured,
not even the poets,
how much a heart can hold.

— ZELDA FITZGERALD

Is that the downward dog pose or are you just worshipping me?

– AUTHOR UNKNOWN

I have a head
for business and
a bod for sin.

– WORKING GIRL
20TH–CENTURY FOX, 1988

There are two kinds of women. . .
you're the worst kind.
You're high maintenance but you
think you're low maintenance.

– WHEN HARRY MET SALLY
COLUMBIA PICTURES, 1989

Love is friendship

set on fire — JEREMY IRONS

I may not be a smart man
but I know what love is.

– FORREST GUMP
PARAMOUNT PICTURES, 1994

The best proof of
love is trust.

— JOYCE BROTHERS

Life has taught us that love does not consist of gazing at each other, but in looking outward together in the same direction.

– ANTOINE DE SAINT-EXUPERY

He's more myself than I am.
Whatever our souls are made of,
his and mine are the same.

– EMILY BRONTË

Be happy.
It's one way
of being wise.

– COLETTE

We waste time looking for the perfect lover, instead of creating the perfect love.

– TOM ROBBINS

The best thing to hold onto in life is each other.

— AUDREY HEPBURN

Happiness often sneaks through a door you didn't know you left open.

— JOHN BARRYMORE

89

We come to love not by finding the perfect person, but by learning to see an imperfect person perfectly.

— ANGELINA JOLIE

And Pooh said to Piglet,
Life is so much friendlier with two.

– A. A. MILNE

"Love means never having to say you're sorry . . ."

That's the dumbest thing
I ever heard.

– WHAT'S UP, DOC?
WARNER BROTHERS, 1972

Real love stories
never have endings.

– RICHARD BACH

It was love at first bite.

– AUTHOR UNKNOWN

Where there is great love
there are always miracles.

– WILLA CATHER

There's language in her eye,
her cheek, her lip.

– WILLIAM SHAKESPEARE

The way is not in the sky.
The way is in the heart.

– BUDDHA

You're my cup of tea.

– AUTHOR UNKNOWN

Embrace your destiny!

– AUTHOR UNKNOWN

*I'll let you be in my dreams
if I can be in yours.*

— BOB DYLAN